Life From My Van:
Poems of a
Semi-Woke Woman

Deborah Howell-Moroney

BookLeaf Publishing

India | USA | UK

Presentation by *BookLeaf Publishing*

Web: www.bookleafpub.com

E-mail: info@bookleafpub.com

ISBN: 9789360947040

First edition 2024

ACKNOWLEDGEMENT

Thank you to Margie S., who coined the phrase "Semi-Woke". She nailed me.
Thank you to Michael, who encourages me and puts up with my compulsions.
My children are my heart. They inspire me every day.

PREFACE

Life is more interesting when you take a breath every once in awhile to take it in. Occasionally to look back and see how far you've come, but, more importantly, to look around yourself and see the beauty and heartbreak, the challenges and the small victories, and not lose yourself in the midst of them. In our ever changing world, it is important to stay "Woke", but as a middle aged white woman, I wonder how to help and not harm. As a person who is always sleepy, it's important to choose wisely. Semi-Woke is a jab at my sleepy attempt to figure out where to best serve and love the world I find myself in.

Combustion

Bursting forth
My atoms commingle with
The newly greened forest
Leaving behind
My skin and bones
Freed from gravity and thought
Existing in new forms
Absorbed.
I look back
At the point of ignition
And I see that
I, too, had a beginning,
But now is
Something
Entirely new

Hero

I imagine I am standing in the grocery store checkout.
Kroger - because it is the end of the month (Whole Foods is strictly a first of the month indulgence)
While I'm nodding off from boredom but trying to keep my face from contorting and jerking,
The cashier- also the manager- rises out of his skin
His head flattens like that of a pit viper
His tongue extends and flicks
He hisses at the woman -who is paying with a check-
"I need to see your ID!!!!"
This is the little Kroger - it once was a Piggly Wiggly, not the big Kroger in the rich neighborhood down the street.
Everyone recognizes everyone else here
We are familiar to each other -like pieces of a quilt
"Hey bottom right corner piece "
"Hey back atcha second from the left near the old baby dress section!"

I immediately think I see the problem. The
manager is new and the customer is
brown-skinned.
I yell, "catch!"
I whip off my skin and throw it over the woman.
The manger pulls his eyeglasses from his head
and puts them on his face.
"Never mind," he says, "have a nice day," he
says. He uncoils himself and shrinks back down
to his former self. Let's pretend he also has a
comb-over, like aging Pete Campbell in the last
season of Mad Men, when he was totally
harmless.
The woman nods to me and throws my skin back
with expert precision. It's a good thing I'd been
in my suburban camouflage, nobody pays
attention to me when I wear it, or they would
have seen my insides. She then walks out the
door with her rotisserie chicken and bottle of
wine.
Actually what happened was:
*The woman immediately puts up her hand
when she sees what I'm doing and says, "I've
got this."
She expertly whips out her drivers license and a
credit card and hands them to tired looking Pete,
who scribbles something down on the check. He
hands back her things and says, "Enjoy your
weekend."

The woman winks at me, twirls, then zooms out
the door and shoots straight into the sky like a
Roman candle. Her family is at home and
h'angry.

* In a surprise twist, the brown-skinned woman
is the hero. This is usually true.

Idling

The space in between
Is neither here
Nor there
Just waiting
Neither the promise nor the past
Just remembering, and yet
The hope of what will be
Is the dawn.

Wishes

Crawling from under a rock
Of condemnation
Of fear
(Self-loathing)
Too soon
(Lets's not go there)
Finding that
As I awaken and emerge
The earth
Did not stop moving on its axis
No one noticed
All the while I wore their clothes
Brushed my teeth
There was no check list
Citation
No black list
No notice of deportation
Barely noticed.
(Stop)
Peering out from under
(No)
Pushing through
(Shhh)
No!
I stretch on tip toe

Arms reaching
Outstretched
Yes!
(Shhh)
Some senses return
Breathe
Inflate
Levitate
Maybe I'm a monster
But it feels like
Wishes.

Autumn

The air so still I barely notice
The rain stopped falling
The misting bark hangs on the tree where
endless dreams were
If only...fades back into days where rushing and
busy stand
derelict, empty
Moving now and barely
sleep, imperative.
Where mingling and isolation blur
I marvel at how little leaves imprint on the
passing time
Indistinct, dissonant
And still I see
That never would it want to be
I'm drawn to days gone
How can it grip yet pass me
Poking, prodding
Most of me has turned into you.
Young eyes shining and I'm longing for home.

Winter

I lay on the white blanket.
Once I stop shivering
I wave my arms high,
Over and down to my waist.
I open and close my legs,
Wide then closed.
I stand, careful not to disturb the angel
Who will never rise.

Wishes 2

Wishes are light beings
No shape or form
Just what might have been
or could be
In dark corners of dreams
Wishes become prayers
And crash to earth
Become things
Taking shape
Taking form
Put on rings
Become finite and mortal
Wishes are like butterfly wings
Do not touch
Born to live at a distance.

A Spark, Then a Flicker

Moving up from the pit
Through the womb
To the place where the spirit resides
A flame
Moving still
Setting fire to the heart
And wants to devour.

Running Errands

I found myself pushing a shopping cart
I wanted to fling it away and walk out
On the way to the door I would put my glass jar
on the counter
The one with a picture of me
And under it in 48 pt Times New Roman would
be the word "MISSING"
In 14 pt the words
"Last seen asleep in her bedroom "
I'd put in one dollar to encourage another
Money draws attention
Maybe I'd return to my cart and continue
shopping
Maybe I'll walk right out the door
Get into my car
And drive to another store
And start over
While trying to decide
Stay or go
I finger the acorn cap in the pocket of my coat
I know how to use it
The secret way to hold it
Wetting my lips
I can blow it and make it whistle
I'm always surprised and pleased with myself

The sound is surprisingly loud
I wonder if I whistled
Who would come?
Maybe it would draw a crowd
They would whisper
That's the woman from the jar
What is she doing here
Where did that sound come from
Or maybe a dog wandering in the parking lot
would run to me and put his foot on mine
I decide the best thing to do is to go back home
and crawl into bed
Just in case someone comes looking

Don't Make Promises

Blink
They're beating the ground they're beating the
ground
The beat in their chests
In time with the sound
They're shaking the ground they're shaking the
ground
We don't make a sound.
A train whistle in the distance
Please take me with you
But how can I get home
When home isn't there
The ground shakes and dissolves
Now I'm falling
Now I'm falling
In slow motion then
No motion
Fullness so empty
Darkness too bright
If fear overtakes me
Will it always be night
The beating in my heart returns
Blood pounding in my head
I'm beating the ground
Outrunning the train
Floating not falling
My eyes close again.

Fatigue

I dreamt I was sitting in a giant cube
As large as a swimming pool
As deep as the one in Beijing
Water started pouring in from some invisible
source
At first I was just annoyed at being wet
Then, as the level started to rise I struggled to
stand on tiptoe so I could breathe
Just before true panic set in
I thought I heard a voice saying, "Use your
superpowers!"
Immediately I turn over on my back and floated
I could breathe
Soon I relaxed and fell into a peaceful slumber
After awhile, the water reached the top, so I
swam to the side and easily stepped out
Sometimes our weakness is our strength

Fresh Batch

I blinked
And it was spring
Had it happened overnight
Robins, heavy with egg,
Lift their wings, flightless.
It was then that
I knew
It was spring
In me, too

Reprise

What if
What could be collides with what is
Two spaces existing simultaneously
And yet one is and one isn't
Hidden in spaces undiscovered
Revealed in a riddle of silence
Maybe forever and never are two sides
Of the same mystery

Wishes 3

Suppose,
It were true
That all and more would come
like a tug, going under
and land like a wild metaphor?
Perhaps,
Nothing will come of it
Except absolution.

DNA

Smile
A smile rises to my lips
Laugh
I summon it from my chest
Because my belly is hollow
Walk
Check
Talk
Check
Breathe
Check
Sleep eludes me
Then it overtakes me
Arise.
Awaken!
Wake up!

Wake up!!

Odyssey

Sitting in my minivan
(I do this a lot)
I was thumping some beats real loud
Flows grinding and voices bumping it
Not the E version, but the one you listen to when
your mom is in the room
My angst is different but also the same
I let the words teach about
The Art of Peer Pressure

Day 'n' Night (Nightmare)

How they do the fingers like Redd Foxx and
about

The Neighbors

If they didn't tell me, I wouldn't know about
making lemons into

Lemonade or

Every Ghetto, Every City

What I hear is

I am needed, but not NEEDED
I should listen, really listen so I'll understand
that
I'll never really understand
Still, it has a great beat and I can dance to it
Maybe the world could use a little more of that.

White Privilege

You can have my skin
If you think it will serve you
It has flaws, but it has served me
It is the shape of a woman
So it comes with a discount
Also, it has aged over 48 years
Some better than others
Still, it provides comfort to children who want a
soft place to rest
My dogs push against its thighs and find peace
I don't really know why its color-
That of infant milk, under-ripe fruit, or a blank
piece of paper -
Is valued over the color of
Smooth milky chocolate
Warm steaming coffee
Rich salty caramel
But I'm told it grants privilege
So, for whatever that's worth,
Please do with it whatever you will.

Offspring

I started singing along to a song on the radio.
My kids start groaning in the back seat. "Mom!
Stop singing!"
I stop singing
After 100,000 gymnastics meets, 350,000 dance
recitals, and eleventy-two parent meetings,
awards assemblies, and graduations from other
than high school.
"That's ok," I say to myself.
"Only I know where the Halloween candy is
hidden."

Desert

Again emerging
This craving
Yearning
Aching
Angst
Like some school girl acting up.

Not happy, not sad
It's just the in-between days that have me down
Can't go forward, but there is no going back.

Try to turn my focus upward
I attempt to direct my thoughts
Through the ceiling, only fleeting
Instead, they move outward
Through the curtains

Call them back
Take them captive
Can not let them find their victim
Still this craving consumes me
A thorn in the flesh

Without understanding
Without my intention

Not Another Word

No fact no opinion
No truth and no fiction
No beauty no poetry
Claims aims ambition
The chains were put on my mouth after they
reached in and cut out my tongue
I can be silenced
Grey turned to ashes
Flesh to stone
A monument to moments
And movements
And monoliths
And monopolies
Singularities and singular things
I could sing but,
Then I would be singular and
We would be me

Napping

I don't want to
Buy something
Go somewhere
I don't want to
Eat or consume
Stay inside or
Go outside
I just want something
Good to happen
Without lifting a finger